99 WaYs To OpeN a BeeR BOttLe WitHout A BottLe OpeNer

99 Ways To Open a Beer Bottle Without A Bottle Opener

brett Stern

Crown Trade Paperbacks   New York

Published by Crown Publishers, Inc., 201 East 50th Street,

New York, New York 10022. Member of the Crown Publishing Group.

Random House, Inc.   New York, Toronto, London, Sydney, Auckland

Crown Trade Paperbacks™ and colophon are trademarks of Crown Publishers, Inc.

Manufactured in the United States of America

Library of Congress Cataloging-in-Publication Data

Stern, Brett.

    99 ways to open a beer bottle without a bottle opener/Brett

Stern. — 1st ed.

      p.   cm.

    1. American wit and humor.   I. Title.   II. Title: Ninety-nine

ways to open a beer bottle without a bottle opener.

PN6162.S825   1993   92-1637

818'.5402 — dc20   CIP

ISBN 0-517-88005-9

10 9 8 7 6 5 4 3 2 1

First Edition

To Mom—

Thanks for keeping the fridge full.

ACKNOWLEDGMENTS

Michael Lucente
Erich Rose
Peter Rivkees
Glenn Rivkees
Michael Cousins
Laura Goodman
Bill Pratt
Erica Marcus
Nancy Yost
Wayne Martens, Box One
   Photographic Services Inc.
Steve Greenberg
Steve Wuesthoff
John Gault
Fran Albin

Alan Mandelbaum
Marko Soccoli, Sam Ash Music
Bobbie Duncan, Sam Ash Music
Frank Badolato
Dan Sabia
Ricardo Spina
Bob Greenfield, North American Trophy
Banu Ogan
Cameron Jenkins
Jeff Lichtenbaum
Robert Wimer
Butch Johnson
Matthew Ingber
Ira Levine

The *tools* by which man, since the beginning of his history, has helped himself to contest with the forces of nature and to supply the needs of his life have always been indispensable servants of his so-called *civilization*.

John Chapman Mercer

1856 – 1930

Imagination is more important than knowledge.

Albert Einstein

1879 – 1955

INTRODUCTION

"Hey, who wants a brew?"

"I do, pass it over. That's nice and cold. Hey, it's not a twist-off. Where's the opener?"

"Check in the kitchen, first drawer on your right."

"Not there."

"Right, I lost that on the camping trip . . . okay, uh, check under the sink."

"Nope."

"Ah, I'll get my trusty Swiss Army knife. Great, I can't find that either."

"Now what?"

We've all been there and know how frustrating it is to have that cold, frosty, thirst-quenching beer in hand and suddenly realize that you can't open it. We cannot always "be prepared" like a Boy Scout, but with this handy "how-to" reference guide, your problems will be solved. You will be able to accomplish this simple task no matter what environment you find yourself in. This manual has examples for a variety of common situations and circumstances that you may encounter. They include:

Home

Office

Sporting Goods

In Your Pockets

Transportation

On the Streets

Tool Box

In Women's Pocketbooks

Last Resort

As you use and apply this information, you will soon realize the variants possible and come up with your own solutions. Let's face it—all you're doing is prying a round piece of metal off a round piece of glass.

To accompany each example, I have instituted a skill-rating system. After the instructions, there is a beer bottle symbol for degree of difficulty.

EASY   MEDIUM   HARD

I wish you luck and happy beer drinking. Always remember:
NEVER DRINK FROM THE BOTTLE IF YOU BREAK THE GLASS!

¹FIRE HYDRANT

1. **FOLLOW ARROW ON TOP—
   "OPEN"**
2. **PLACE CAP IN RECESS
   BETWEEN SCREW AND NUT**
3. **PRESS DOWN**
4. **DRINK**

°CAR DOOR LATCH

1. OPEN DOOR
2. PLACE CAP IN OPENING
3. PRESS FORWARD
4. DRINK

³Pipe Wrench

1. **OPEN JAWS ABOUT AN INCH**
2. **PRESS DOWN**
3. **DRINK**

⁴BABY CARRIAGE

1. TAKE BABY OUT FOR A STROLL

2. PLACE CAP AS SHOWN

3. DRINK

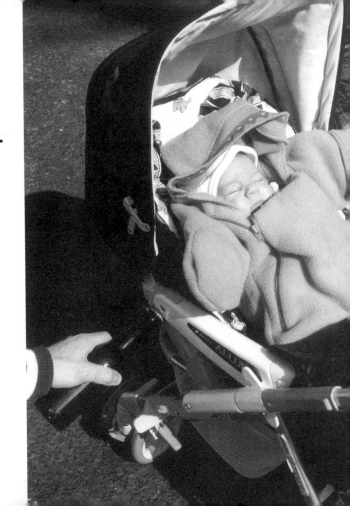

°Police Car

1. **MAKE SURE NOBODY IS IN THE CAR**
2. **PLACE CAP IN TRUNK LID**
3. **PRESS DOWN**
4. **DRINK**
5. **DON'T GET CAUGHT**

STREET SIGNS

1. **WEDGE CAP IN METAL STRAP**
2. **PRESS DOWN**
3. **DRINK**

°ICE SKATES

1. **PLACE CAP IN OPENING**
2. **PRESS DOWN**
3. **DRINK**

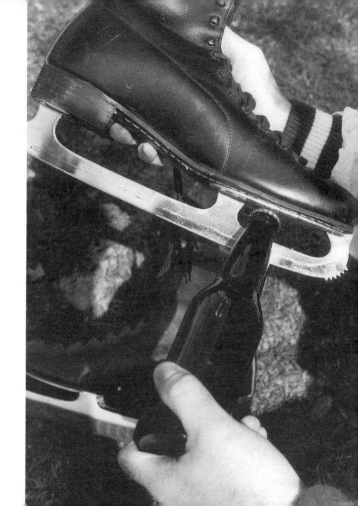

°8 TRUCK

1. **PLACE CAP IN TAILGATE**
2. **PRESS DOWN**
3. **DRINK**

GARBAGE CAN

1. **WEDGE CAP IN METAL FRAME**
2. **PRESS DOWN**
3. **DRINK**
4. **DON'T THROW BOTTLE AWAY—**
   RECYCLE

DOLLY

1. **HOLD WHEEL**
2. **PLACE CAP IN WHEEL SUPPORT**
3. **PRESS DOWN**
4. **DRINK**

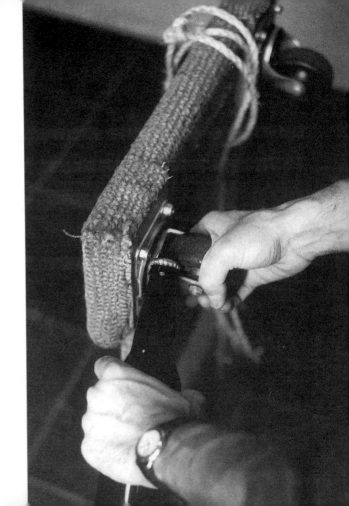

¹¹ GARAGE DOOR

1. **PLACE CAP IN SLOT OF DOOR RAIL**
2. **PRESS DOWN**
3. **DRINK**

¹²Bathroom Stall Hinge

1. **YOU'RE IN THE BATHROOM BECAUSE YOU'VE ALREADY HAD A FEW**
2. **PLACE CAP IN DOOR HINGE**
3. **PRESS DOWN**
4. **GO BACK TO PARTY**
5. **DRINK**

SAVE

REPORT LEAKS
CALL SUPT. OR
(212) 3_
Call: (212

⑬ LADDER

1. **GET OFF LADDER**
2. **PLACE CAP IN CORNER BRACE**
3. **PRESS DOWN**
4. **DRINK**
5. **DON'T GET BACK ON LADDER**

¹⁴ PUBLIC TELEPHONE

1. **PICK UP RECEIVER AND PRETEND TO TALK TO SOMEONE**
2. **PLACE CAP IN COIN RETURN**
3. **PRESS DOWN**
4. **DRINK**

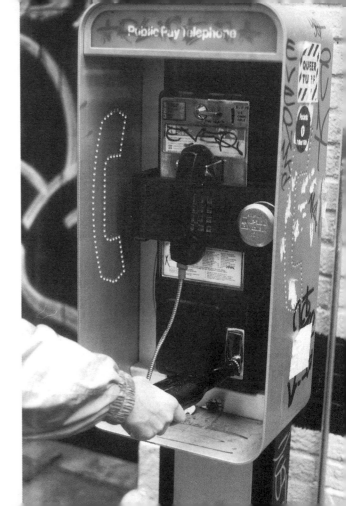

Guitar

1. "TAKE FIVE" FROM PLAYING
2. PLACE EDGE OF CAP ON BRIDGE
3. PULL DOWN
4. DRINK

LAWN MOWER

1. **PLACE CAP IN BETWEEN METAL AND WHEEL**
2. **PRESS DOWN**
3. **DRINK**
4. **NOW GET BACK TO WORK**

BICYCLE GEARS

1. **WEDGE CAP IN GEARS**
2. **PRESS DOWN**
3. **DRINK**
4. **DON'T RIDE**

18 SHOVEL

1. **PLACE CAP IN BETWEEN HANDLE AND SHOVEL BLADE**
2. **PRESS DOWN**
3. **DRINK**

¹⁹SCAFFOLD

1. **PLACE CAP IN BETWEEN PIPE AND SUPPORT**
2. **PRESS DOWN**
3. **DRINK**

FILE CABINET

1. **PLACE CAP IN DRAWER PULL**
2. **PRESS DOWN**
3. **HIDE FROM BOSS**
4. **DRINK**

²¹NAIL CLIPPER

1. PLACE CLIPPER PART
   UNDER CAP
2. LIFT UP
3. DRINK

22 Seat Belt Strap

1. **PLACE METAL CATCH OVER CAP RIM**

2. **TWIST OFF**

3. **DRINK***

***DRINKING AND DRIVING DON'T MIX**

23 STANDPIPE

1. PLACE CAP IN METAL LIP
2. PRESS DOWN
3. DRINK

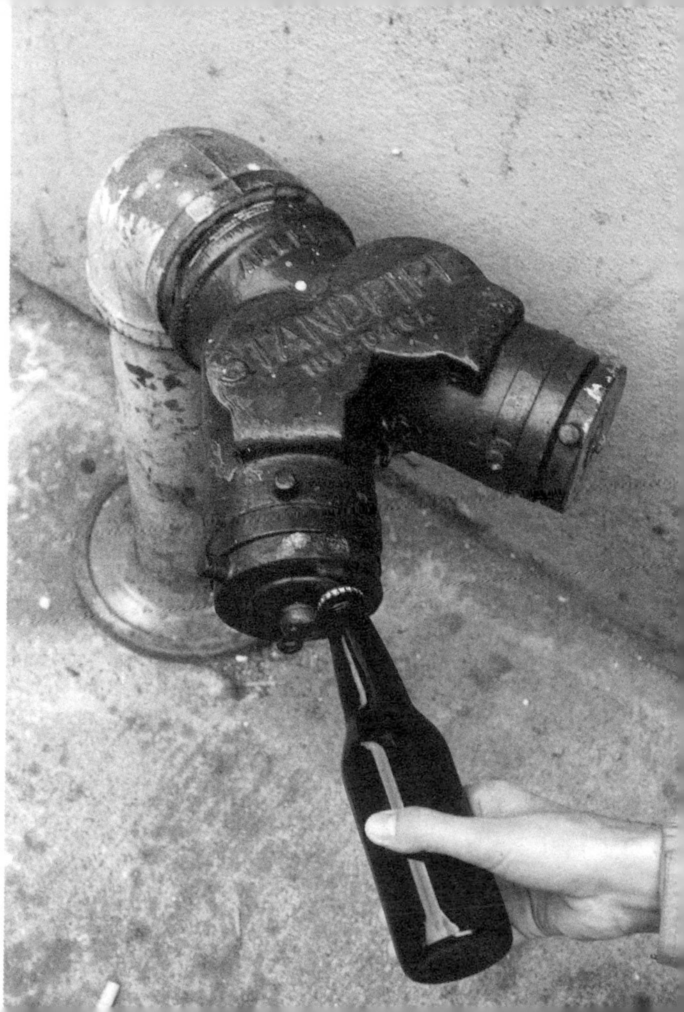

POLICE/FIRE CALL BOX

[24]

1. **LIFT METAL DOOR**
2. **PLACE CAP IN BACK HINGE**
3. **PRESS DOWN**
4. **DRINK**
5. **DON'T BE DUMB AND PUSH THE BUTTON**

Eyelash Curler

1. **PLACE METAL LIP UNDER CAP**
2. **GENTLY LIFT UP**
3. **DRINK**

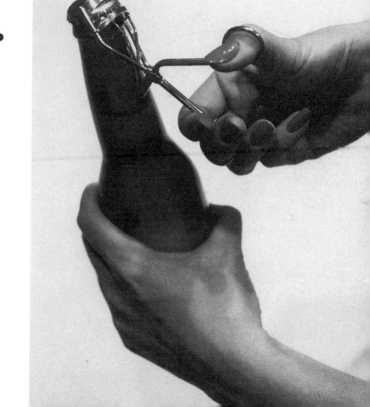

GUARD RAIL

1. **PLACE CAP IN SLOT**

2. **PRESS DOWN**

3. **DRINK**

27

Barbecue Grill

1. STICK CAP IN GRILL
2. PRESS DOWN
3. DRINK
4. DON'T FORGET TO FLIP THE BURGERS

²⁸Streetlight Pole

1. **PLACE CAP IN BETWEEN SCREW AND NUT**
2. **PRESS DOWN**
3. **DRINK**

STAPLER

1. **CLOSE OFFICE DOOR**
2. **PLACE CAP IN STAPLER AS SHOWN**
3. **PRESS DOWN**
4. **DRINK**

³⁰NAIL FILE

1. HOLD BOTTLE SECURELY
2. PRY OFF CAP
3. MAKE SURE YOU DON'T
   BREAK A NAIL
4. DRINK

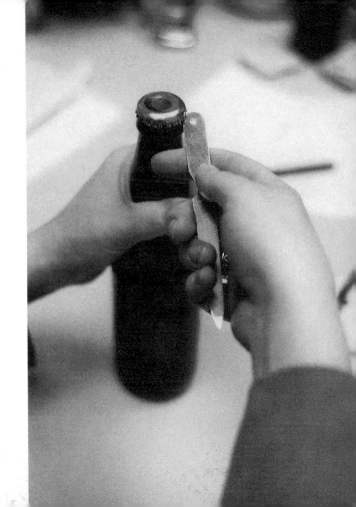

MAIL STORAGE BOX

1. PLACE CAP BETWEEN DOOR
   AND METAL RIM

2. PRESS DOWN

3. DRINK

HAMMER

1. PLACE CLAW UNDER CAP LIP

2. PRY OFF

3. DRINK

[33] Bicycle Brake Handle

1. **RIDE TWENTY-FIVE MILES**
2. **SQUEEZE BRAKE HANDLE**
3. **PLACE CAP IN OPENING**
4. **PRESS DOWN**

³⁴TOILET

1. **PLACE CAP IN BETWEEN VALVE AND PIPE**
2. **PRESS DOWN**
3. **DRINK**

³⁵DOOR LOCK

1. **PLACE CAP IN OPENING**
2. **LIFT UP**
3. **DRINK**

GOLF CLUB

1. **SELECT IRON OF YOUR CHOICE**
2. **PLACE THUMB ON CAP FOR LEVERAGE**
3. **PLACE CLUB UNDER CAP**
4. **PRESS UP WITH CLUB AND DOWN WITH THUMB**
5. **DRINK**
6. **PLAY ANOTHER 18**

Ticket Booth Speaker Grill

1. **SHOVE CAP INTO GRILL**
2. **PRESS DOWN**
3. **DRINK**

³⁸SLED

1. **PLACE CAP IN BETWEEN METAL BARS**
2. **PRESS DOWN**
3. **DRINK**

BICYCLE WHEEL

1. **PLACE CAP IN BETWEEN SPOKES**
2. **GENTLY PRY OFF**
3. **DRINK**

⁴⁰VICE

1. **OPEN VICE ABOUT ¼ INCH**
2. **WEDGE CAP IN OPENING**
3. **PRESS DOWN**
4. **DRINK**

⁴¹WATER VALVE

1. **PLACE CAP IN BETWEEN HANDLE AND PIPE**
2. **PRESS DOWN**
3. **DRINK**

⁴²METAL GATE

1. PLACE CAP IN BETWEEN FRAME AND DOOR

2. TWIST

3. DRINK

SAXOPHONE

1. **BLOW A FEW TUNES**
2. **PLACE CAP UNDER RIM OF HORN BELL**
3. **PRY OFF**
4. **DRINK**
5. **PLAY SOME MORE**

POOL BRIDGE

1. HOLD BRIDGE NEAR THE END
2. PLACE CAP IN OPENING
3. PRESS DOWN
4. DON'T SPILL ANY ON THE TABLE
5. DRINK

⁴⁵Scissors

1. **PLACE BOTH POINTS INTO CAP**
2. **PRY OFF WITHOUT STABBING SELF**
3. **DRINK**

TAPE MEASURE

1. PLACE METAL TAB UNDER CAP
2. KEEP TAPE INSIDE HOUSING
3. PRY OFF
4. DRINK

⁴⁷LOCK SHACKLE

1. **UNLOCK DOOR**
2. **PLACE CAP IN OPENING**
3. **PRESS DOWN**
4. **LOCK DOOR**
5. **DRINK**

ELEVATOR

1. **PLACE CAP IN BETWEEN DOOR AND CAB FRAME**
2. **PULL BACK**
3. **DON'T FORGET TO PUSH A FLOOR BUTTON**
4. **DRINK**

⁴⁹Letter Opener

1. PLACE POINT INTO CAP

2. PRY OPEN BY TWISTING
POINT AROUND ENTIRE CAP

3. DRINK

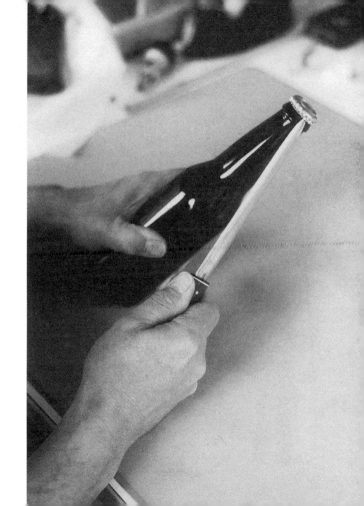

50 NAPKIN DISPENSER

1. HOLD DISPENSER SECURELY

2. PLACE CAP IN OPENING

3. PRESS DOWN

4. DRINK

TROPHY

1. PLACE CAP IN BETWEEN THE
LEGS OF ONLY TROPHY YOU
EVER WON*

2. BEND OFF

3. DRINK

4. CONTINUE STORY ABOUT HOW
YOU WON THE GAME

*MUST BE METAL TROPHY

CAMERA

1. PLACE CAP IN FLASH CLIP

2. PRY OFF CAP GENTLY

3. DRINK

METAL FENCE

1. **FIND DECORATIVE METAL ON FENCE**
2. **PLACE CAP WHERE APPROPRIATE**
3. **PRESS DOWN**
4. **DRINK**

Mail Slot

1. PUSH CAP INTO MAIL SLOT
2. PRESS DOWN
3. DRINK

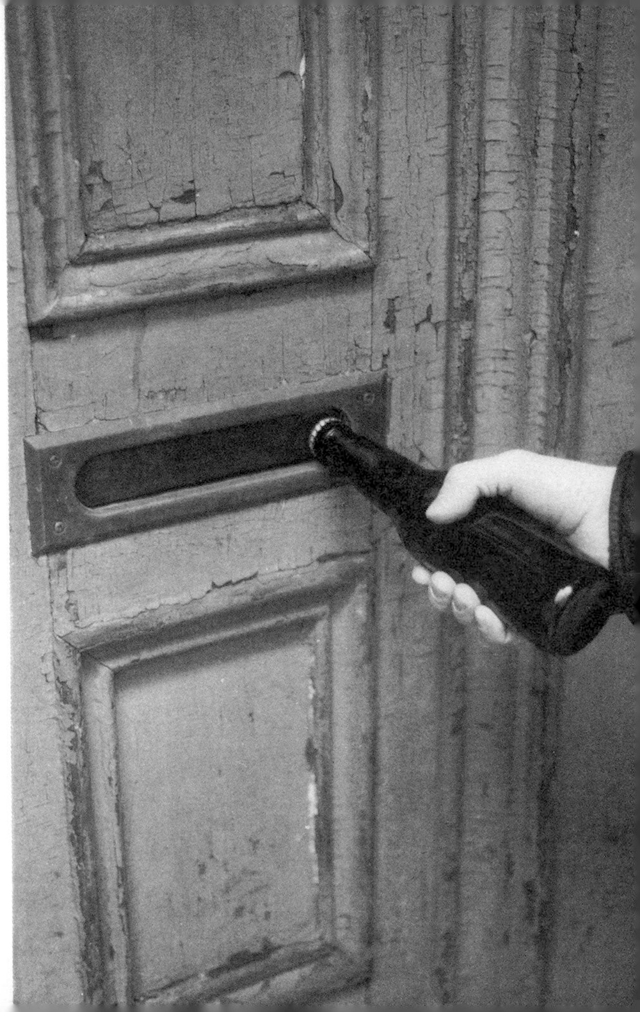

⁵⁵PLIERS

1. HEY, STUPID! JUST LOOK AT
THE PICTURE

Dog Collar

1. HOLD BOTTLE AND DOG SECURELY
2. PLACE DOG LICENSE TAG UNDER CAP RIM
3. PRY OFF
4. DRINK
5. FINISH WALKING DOG

Corkscrew

1. **PLACE POINT OF SCREW UNDER RIM**
2. **PRY OFF**
3. **DRINK**

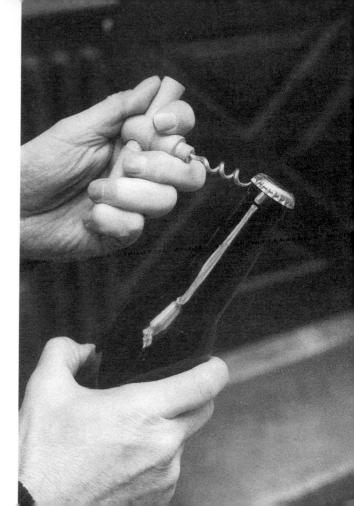

Roof Parapet

1. **GO UP TO ROOF**
2. **WEDGE CAP IN BETWEEN BRICKS**
3. **BEND OFF CAP**
4. **DRINK**

EDGE OF TABLE

1. **PLACE CAP ON EDGE OF TABLE**
2. **JUST PUNCH THE *#!$ OUT OF IT**
3. **DRINK THE REWARDS**

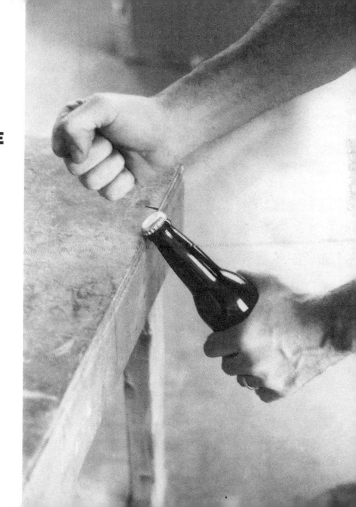

60 GATE

1. PLACE CAP IN BETWEEN METAL BARS
2. PRESS DOWN
3. DRINK

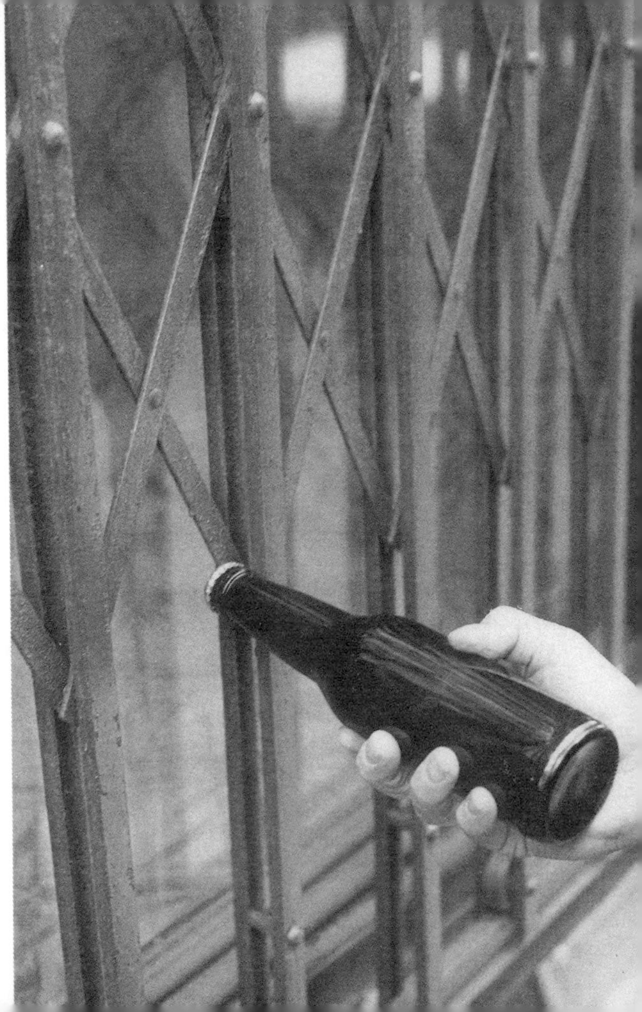

⁶¹VAN DOOR HINGE

1. **PLACE CAP IN BETWEEN HINGE AND DOOR**
2. **PRESS DOWN**
3. **DRINK**

DISPOSABLE LIGHTER

1. **HOLD BOTTLE AS SHOWN**
2. **PLACE BOTTOM OF LIGHTER UNDER CAP**
3. **PULL LIGHTER UP**
4. **DRINK**

FOR PROS ONLY

WHEEL

1. **FIND A WHEEL OR HUBCAP WITH SLOT**
2. **INSERT CAP IN GROOVE**
3. **PRESS DOWN**
4. **DRINK**

Newspaper Vending Machine

1. **PRETEND TO READ HEADLINES**
2. **PLACE CAP IN COIN RETURN**
3. **PRESS DOWN**
4. **DRINK**

COMPUTER

1. PLACE CAP IN HARD DRIVE SLOT
2. PRY OFF CAREFULLY
3. DRINK
4. PLAY SOME MORE COMPUTER GAMES

NOTE: THIS WILL PROBABLY SCRATCH YOUR COMPUTER, BUT IT WILL OPEN YOUR BEER

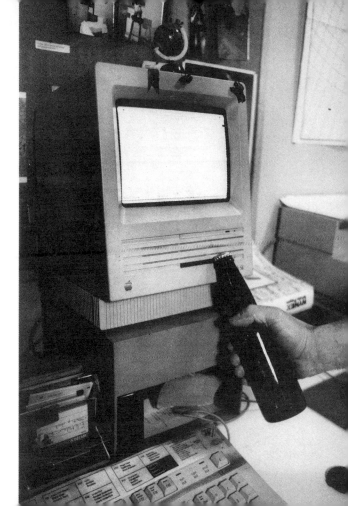

TAPE DISPENSER

1. GO TO STOCKROOM SO NOBODY WILL FIND YOU

2. PLACE CAP IN METAL CUTOUT

3. TWIST OFF

4. DRINK

BOTTLE TO BOTTLE

1. **HOLD CAP TO CAP**
2. **PULL APART, TRYING TO GET THE BOTTOM BOTTLE TO OPEN FIRST**
3. **DRINK**

NOTE: **DUE TO MURPHY'S LAW, THE TOP BOTTLE USUALLY OPENS FIRST, SO ADJUST ACCORDINGLY**

Bank Night Drop-off Box

1. **PLACE CAP IN BETWEEN METAL SURFACES**
2. **PRESS DOWN**
3. **DRINK**

⁶⁹WIRE CUTTERS

1. HOLD BOTTLE SECURELY

2. GENTLY PRY OFF CAP

3. DRINK

70 Catcher's Mask

1. PLACE CAP IN WIRE FRAME
2. PRY OFF
3. REMEMBER TO TAKE OFF MASK
4. DRINK

NOTE: THIS WILL ALSO WORK WITH FOOTBALL HELMET AND HOCKEY MASK

⁷¹ CASH MACHINE

1. **PLACE CAP IN CASH DISPENSER SLOT**
2. **PULL UP**
3. **DRINK**
4. **TAKE OUT TEN BUCKS TO GET MORE BEER**

PAPER TOWEL DISPENSER

1. **PLACE CAP IN METAL OPENING**
2. **PRESS DOWN**
3. **PULL OUT PAPER TOWEL TO WIPE UP SPILLED BEER**
4. **DRINK**

ENGINE

1. **PLACE CAP IN ANY AVAILABLE SLOT**
2. **PULL FORWARD**
3. **DRINK***

*DRINKING AND DRIVING DON'T MIX

Dumpster

1. **ON SOMETHING THIS BIG IT HAS TO WORK SOMEWHERE**
2. **DRINK**

ROLLER BLADES

1. PLACE CAP IN BETWEEN

SHOE AND BLADE

2. PRY OFF

3. DRINK

LOCKER

76

1. **OPEN DOOR**
2. **PLACE CAP IN OPENING**
3. **PULL UP**
4. **CLOSE DOOR**
5. **DRINK**

77 Peanut Vending Machine

1. PLACE CAP IN COIN SLOT
2. PRESS DOWN
3. DRINK

ZIPPER

1. **UNDO ZIPPER**
2. **PRY OFF WITH METAL TAB**
3. **DRINK**
4. **REMEMBER TO ZIP YOUR FLY**

⁷⁹PEN

1. **FIND A METAL PEN — PLASTIC WILL BREAK**
2. **PLACE POINT UNDER CAP**
3. **PRY OFF**
4. **DRINK**
5. **FINISH WRITING THE TERM PAPER**

⁸⁰HAND DRYER

1. PLACE CAP IN BETWEEN
DRYER BODY AND
PUSH-BUTTON

2. PRY OFF

3. DRINK

⁸¹NAIL

1. **BEND NAIL DOWN**
2. **STICK CAP UNDER HEAD OF NAIL**
3. **PRESS DOWN ON BOTTLE**
4. **DRINK**

⁸²WHEELCHAIR

1. **HOLD BEER SECURELY**
2. **PRY OFF CAP AGAINST METAL FRAME**
3. **DRINK**

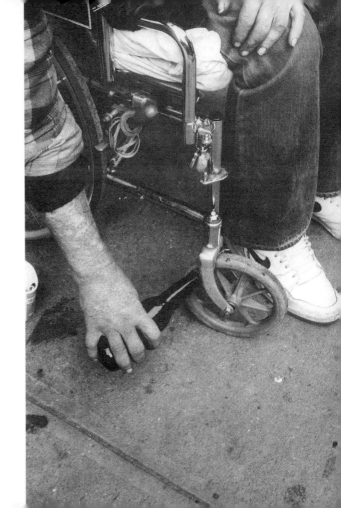

DUMBBELL

1. **FINISH TWENTY REPS**
2. **PLACE CAP IN BETWEEN WEIGHT AND COLLAR**
3. **BEND OFF**
4. **DRINK**
5. **DO TWENTY MORE REPS**

⁸⁴ Folding Chair

1. PLACE CAP IN HINGE AREA
2. PULL UP
3. DRINK

NOTE: THIS WORKS WELL ON
BEACH CHAIRS, TOO

SCREWDRIVER

1. **WEDGE SCREWDRIVER TIP UNDER CAP**
2. **PRY OFF**
3. **DRINK**

Laundry Dryer

1. **COLLECT ONE MONTH'S WORTH OF DIRTY CLOTHES**
2. **WASH AND DRY**
3. **STICK CAP IN DRYER DOOR HINGE AND PRESS DOWN**
4. **DRINK**
5. **WAIT FOR CLOTHES TO DRY**

SKATEBOARD

1. **PLACE CAP BETWEEN AXLE AND SCREW**
2. **PRESS DOWN**
3. **DRINK**

Chain Link Fence

1. **PLACE CAP IN BETWEEN FENCE AND METAL BAR**
2. **PRESS DOWN**
3. **DRINK**

BELT BUCKLE

1. **UNDO BUCKLE (DON'T LET PANTS FALL)**
2. **ADJUST BUCKLE ACCORDINGLY**
3. **PRY OFF**
4. **DRINK**
5. **DON'T FORGET TO BUCKLE UP**

DRUMS

1. **PLAY A FIVE-MINUTE SOLO**
2. **PLACE CAP IN BETWEEN DRUM AND METAL LUG**
3. **PRESS DOWN**
4. **DRINK**

IN/OUT BASKET

1. **FILE SOME PAPERS**
2. **PLACE CAP IN WIRE FRAME**
3. **BEND OFF**
4. **DRINK**
5. **FILE SOME MORE PAPERS**

SKI BINDING

1. **SKI ALL DAY**
2. **GO TO LODGE**
3. **LEAN SKI AGAINST WALL**
4. **PLACE BEER IN TOE BINDING**
5. **PRESS DOWN**
6. **DRINK**

KEY

1. **PLACE END OF KEY UNDER CAP**
2. **PRY OFF**
3. **DRINK**

HOOD ORNAMENT

1. **FIND AN OLD PICK-UP TRUCK**
2. **PLACE CAP IN MUSTANG'S MOUTH (ANY ANIMAL WILL DO)**
3. **PRESS DOWN**
4. **DRINK**

⁹⁵KITCHEN KNIFE

1. **PLACE BLADE OF KNIFE UNDER CAP**
2. **PRY OFF**
3. **DRINK**

NOTE: **A SPOON OR FORK WILL ALSO WORK**

ROOF DRAIN

1. **PLACE CAP IN DRAIN COVER**
2. **PRY OFF**
3. **DON'T SPILL ANY DOWN DRAIN**
4. **DRINK**

TENNIS NET

1. **PLAY THREE SETS OF TENNIS**
2. **PLACE BEER IN NET TENSION CRANK**
3. **PRESS DOWN**
4. **DRINK**

MOTORCYCLE

1. **PLACE CAP IN CYLINDER BLOCK**
2. **PRESS DOWN**
3. **DRINK, BUT DON'T DRIVE**
4. **WEAR A HELMET**

⁹⁹TEETH

1. **MUST BE TOTALLY DESPERATE**
2. **PLACE CAP INSIDE MOUTH**
3. **BITE OFF (BE CAREFUL*)**
4. **DRINK AND ENJOY**

*REMEMBER KIDS—

DON'T TRY THIS AT HOME!

Got a better idea? Let me know.

Brett Stern, author
c/o Crown Publishers, Inc.
201 East 50th Street, 5-3
New York, NY 10022